THE Mystery OF THE Egyptian Mummy

JOYCE FILER

OXFORD

UNIVERSITY PRESS

In association with the British Museum

Contents

This book is dedicated with love to Ted and Rikki Barritt.

Grateful thanks to: Suzan Aral at Jeffery Design for her excellent design work; Jim Stanton for designing a wonderful cover; Claire Thorne for drawing the skull and hip bones; Tania Watkins for help throughout the project; Margot Rentoul, Paul Smith for radiography; Barry Chandler, Antony Reynolds, and Sean Goldner for CAT scan images and advice; Carol Andrews, Joann Fletcher, Nigel Strudwick for supplying photos; Sandra Marshall for skillful photography; Richard Neave and Denise Smith for the models on page 24; Carol Andrews, Richard Parkinson, Neal Spencer, and Stephen Quirke for advice; The Honeybon family; Cassie and Nicole Suleyman-Hall and Isabelle Lemberger-Cooper for help with photos; Carmen Lange, Patricia Neville, and Mary Power for advice; Ted and Rikki Barritt for support.

Last, but certainly not least, an enormous thank you to Carolyn Jones, a wonderful editor with an enticing supply of sweets!

Illustration acknowledgments:

Photographs are taken by the British Museum Photography & Imaging Department, © the Trustees of the British Museum, unless otherwise stated.

Carol Andrews: 23 top
BFI Collections: 15 left.
Frances Button: front cover illustration of Hornedjitef.
stéphanecompoint.com: 22 bottom.
The Griffith Institute, Oxford: 14 top left.
Graham Harrison: 7 bottom, 26 top right, 28 top right.
From Flinders Petrie: *A Life in Archaeology* by Margaret Drower (Victor Gollancz): 13 top.
Joyce Filer: 4 bottom, 7 top right, 10 top right, 11 right, 12 top left, 13 bottom (with the kind permission of Girton College); 14 top right, 15 top right, 15 bottom, 16 top right, 17 top and center, 18 top, 18 bottom left, 19 top left, 19 bottom right, 20 bottom, 21 bottom left, 24 top right, 25 bottom center and bottom right, 26 bottom left, 27 bottom left, 31 top left, 31 bottom right, 33, 34, 37 bottom left and right, 41 top left.
Joann Fletcher, 31 bottom left.
The Metropolitan Museum of Art, Rogers Fund 1920. (20.2.21). Photograph © 1986 The Metropolitan Museum of Art: 30 bottom left.
Peter Nahum at The Leicester Galleries: 16 bottom left.
© The Museum of Mediterranean and Near Eastern Antiquities, Stockholm. Photograph: Ove Kaneberg: 5 top center.
Princess Grace Hospital: 35 (main picture), 37 top center, 38 bottom right, 39 top and center.
Christophe Ratier/NHPA: 18 bottom right.
Red-Head Photography: 27 top.
Rijksmuseum van Oudheden, Leiden: 44 top left.
Roemer und Pelizaeus Museum, Hildesheim, Germany: 9 top right.
Staatliche Sammlung Agyptischer Kunst, Munich: 21 right.
Claire Thorne: 23 bottom right (map) 24 bottom right (map); 36 (bone drawings).

Timeline of ancient Egypt

(*c.* in a date is short for the Latin word *circa*, which means "around")

© 2003 Joyce Filer

First published in 2003 by
The British Museum Press
A division of The British
Museum Company Ltd
46 Bloomsbury Street,
London WC1B 3QQ

Published in the United States
of America by
Oxford University Press, Inc.
198 Madison Avenue
New York, NY 10016
www.oup.com

Oxford is a registered
trademark of Oxford
University Press, Inc.

ISBN 0-19-521989-9 lib. ed.
ISBN 0-19-521990-2 trade ed.

Library of Congress
Cataloging-in-Publication
data is available.

Designed and typeset by
Jeffery Design.
Printed and bound in Hong
Kong by C&C Offset.

5500–3100 BC	Predynastic period
2686–2181 BC	Old Kingdom
2181–2055 BC	First intermediate period
2055–1650 BC	Middle Kingdom
1650–1550 BC	Second intermediate period
1550–1069 BC	New Kingdom

18th Dynasty	*c. 1539–c. 1292 BC*
Amenhotep III	1390–1352 BC
Tutankhamun	*c. 1333–1323 BC*
19th Dynasty	*c. 1292–c. 1190 BC*
Sety I	1294–1279 BC
Ramesses II	1279–1213 BC
Ramesses III	1184–1153 BC

1069–747 BC	Third intermediate period
747–332 BC	Late period (including two invasions by Persians)

26th Dynasty 667–525 BC
Herodotus (*c.* 485–425 BC), Greek historian, visits Egypt
Alexander the Great (356–323 BC)

332–30 BC	Ptolemaic period (when Hornedjitef lived)

332 BC Alexander conquers Egypt

331 BC Alexandria founded

Ptolemy I Soter	*c.* 367–283 BC
Ptolemy III Euergetes	246–222 BC
Ptolemy IV Philopator	222–204 BC
Ptolemy V Epiphanes	204–181 BC
Rosetta Stone	196 BC
Cleopatra	51–30 BC

30 BC – AD 395	Roman period

1 Who was Hornedjitef?

This book is about an ancient Egyptian man named Hornedjitef (say this 'Hor-ned-jit-af'). Hornedjitef's mummy is now in the British Museum.

Hornedjitef was a real man who lived over 2,000 years ago in ancient Egypt, in a city called Thebes (now the modern city of Luxor). He held a high-status job as a priest during the time when the Greeks ruled Egypt, and when he died he was buried with full honors in a **tomb** in the Asasif area of Thebes.

Hornedjitef's titles were written on his coffin, and they tell us that he was a priest of the god Amun in the temple at Karnak. His name means "Horus who avenges his father," in memory of the god Horus.

After Hornedjitef died his body was mummified and put into two coffins, one inside the other. Both coffins were placed in a tomb. Various objects were put in the tomb with his body. They were a **papyrus** roll, a hardened linen sun-disc to keep the mummy warm, a storage box meant to hold internal organs, and a wooden statue of a god who would help the mummy reach the afterlife.

We no longer know exactly where in the Asasif area of Thebes his tomb was, but by looking at tombs of other priests of Amun of the same time we can tell what it must have been like. All the people who were involved in finding Hornedjitef's tomb have been dead a long time themselves.

The temple at Karnak. Hornedjitef may have walked by these tall columns as he went about his work.

The inner coffin of an ancient Egyptian man named Nesiau (now in Stockholm). It is very much like Hornedjitef's coffin, which you can see on page 42.

Other burials of the period were probably similar to that of Hornedjitef. The mummy of another priest, called Ankh-hor, was found at Asasif in a tomb from earlier times. There is also another coffin, similar in style to Hornedjitef's inner coffin, in a museum in Stockholm, Sweden.

Hornedjitef probably had a reasonably-sized tomb in the Asasif. The tomb was not likely to have been damaged by water or falling rocks. We can say this because his mummy and tomb goods are in such good condition.

Mr Henry Salt.

This is the title page from the Sotheby's catalog in which Hornedjitef's mummy and his tomb goods were listed for sale in 1835.

The consul-general's collection

If Hornedjitef lived, worked, and was buried in ancient Thebes, how did he come to be lying in a glass case in the British Museum? Many of the Egyptian objects in the museum came from the collection of Henry Salt (1780–1827). From 1815 Henry Salt was the British consul-general in Egypt. He spent a lot of time there excavating and collecting objects for the British Museum and for himself. In 1835 one of Salt's collections was brought to London by Giovanni d'Athanasi, who worked with Henry Salt, and sold by Sotheby's auction house in London.

That same assistant wrote a catalog about some of Salt's collections, and about the mummy of Hornedjitef he wrote: "it is the finest in quality of all that have ever been found in Thebes."

Mummy for sale

The British Museum bought the mummy of Hornedjitef and the objects from his tomb in this sale. Records show that they cost about $500.

By studying these objects from Hornedjitef's tomb we can also find out about his work as a priest and about the beliefs and religion of the people who lived in Egypt when he was alive.

If we look carefully at his mummy we can make the most important discoveries of all—we can learn about the man Hornedjitef himself. Finding out about a person who lived a long time ago is an archaeological story and also a detective story. We will use some very modern ways of finding out about Hornedjitef's life.

Hornedjitef has kept his secrets for more than 2,000 years but now it is time to reveal them in *The Mystery of the Egyptian Mummy!*

2 Uncovering the secrets of mummification

ornedjitef's mummy is a very fine example of the practice of mummification, a kind of **embalming**. However, it is important to remember that the ancient Egyptians were only able to make mummies of such high quality after hundreds of years of experimentation and practice.

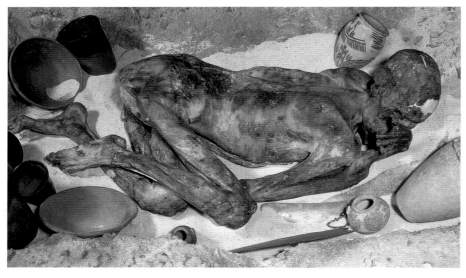

This sand-dried body is an excellent example of a natural mummy. He is nicknamed "Ginger" because of the color of his hair.

Natural mummies

Before they started to bury their dead as deliberately-made mummies, the ancient Egyptians buried people in the hot desert sands. The extreme heat of the sand quickly dried out the bodies, helping to preserve them. In many cases most of the body survived: skin, hair, teeth, and bones. These sand-dried bodies are described as "naturally mummified." Often strong winds or burrowing animals shifted the sands, allowing sand-dried bodies to be revealed. It is possible that the amazing sight of these preserved bodies made the ancient Egyptians think and ask questions about what happened after death.

Reaching the afterlife

Why did the Egyptians mummify their dead? The Egyptians believed that, after they died, people would go on a journey to an afterlife where they would be born again. To make sure this second life happened, the Egyptians thought it was essential that the dead person's body was preserved. The rule seems to be "no body, no afterlife!" Obviously, people wanted the same things in the afterlife that they had in this life, so family and friends provided the dead person with food, animal skin coverings, pottery, and other things. At first these goods were put with the body in reed baskets or simple wooden boxes but this caused a

A burial at Hierakonpolis, from about 3,400 BC. The skin and hair have not survived, because the body wasn't buried deep enough in the hot desert sands.

Once this body was put in a wooden box away from the hot Egyptian sands the skin, muscles and hair decayed, leaving it as a skeleton.

problem. Once the dead bodies were put in boxes or under animal skins they were no longer in contact with the drying effects of the hot desert sands and so the skin, muscles, and hair decayed. This also happened when the dead were buried in tombs. So the Egyptians had to think of a way of providing the dead with goods but at the same time stopping the bodies from decaying. Perhaps they thought about the good preservation of sand-dried bodies and experimented with ways of copying this method of preserving bodies. They needed a substance that mimicked the drying-out action of hot sand. At last they found the answer—salt!

Making mummies deliberately

We know that the Egyptians were trying to preserve bodies deliberately during the Old Kingdom period. The newest evidence from archaeological excavations suggests that they were trying to do this much earlier than experts had first thought. Some of the naturally sand-dried bodies from the **predynastic cemetery** at Hierakonpolis, for example, were found wrapped in pads and strips of linen. It is also possible that the Egyptians were using resin as part of the mummification process at this time.

During the time of the **Old Kingdom**, when the great pyramids at Giza were built, further attempts were made to preserve bodies. Layers of linen and **gypsum** were wrapped around the body and allowed to dry. Sometimes the features of the face— eyes, eyebrows, and hair—were painted on this solid casing in black paint. However, nothing was done to stop the body inside from rotting, so many of these Old Kingdom "mummies" were little more than plaster statues with loose bones inside.

Better mummy-making

The Egyptians continued to try and improve their mummification skills into the Middle Kingdom period, but the quality of these mummies varies. Some were fairly successfully preserved but many were not. Some like Ankhef, a mummy in the British Museum, are little more than a skeleton beneath an elaborately-painted face cover. Reports from early 20th-century excavations note that some Middle Kingdom mummies crumbled when touched.

The mummy of Ankhef is really just a skeleton covered with linen.

A knife used to cut open bodies during the process of mummification. The blade is made of flint.

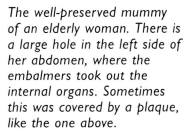

The well-preserved mummy of an elderly woman. There is a large hole in the left side of her abdomen, where the embalmers took out the internal organs. Sometimes this was covered by a plaque, like the one above.

Slowing down decay

It was only during the **New Kingdom** period that the ancient Egyptians produced the better-quality mummies. First, the embalmers laid the dead person on an embalming table. One of them used a flint knife to make a cut in the left side of the **abdomen**, between the ribs and hip bones. He then put his hand inside the body and took out all the internal organs, except the heart. By this time, the Egyptians had realized that it was the internal organs, such as the lungs, liver, intestines, and stomach, that started the rotting process in a dead body. If they removed these organs, decay would be slowed down. The organs were sometimes put in separate pots called **canopic jars**.

Four canopic jars. These were made during the 21st dynasty, many years before Hornedjitef lived.

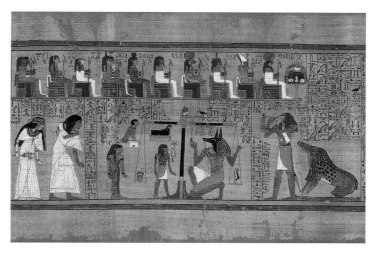

The "weighing of the heart" ceremony, from a papyrus belonging to a man named Ani. Ani's heart is being weighed against the feather of truth, to see if he had been a good or bad person. The god Anubis is supervising the weighing.

These scenes of mummification are painted on a mummy case now in Germany. You can see Anubis, the god of embalming, looking after the body of a man named Djed Bastet-Iuf while it is being mummified.

The Egyptians believed the heart controlled speech and thought and was therefore the body's most important organ. They also believed the person would need the heart when he or she was judged before the gods in the next life so it was left inside the body. A long metal hook was pushed up the nose, breaking through the bones into the skull case, allowing the brain to be pulled out. The Egyptians did not think the brain was important, so it was not kept. On some occasions the skull was packed with linen or resin, but sometimes it was left empty. The body was cleaned and packed with bags of natron, a kind of salt found in certain parts of Egypt. Then the whole body was covered with a pile of natron that **dessicated** the body in the same way as the hot sands did for naturally-dried mummies. The natron also killed off any **bacteria** that might cause the body to decay.

The Greek reporter

How long did it take to make a mummy in ancient Egypt? The problem is that while the ancient Egyptians wrote about many things on **papyrus** and painted many scenes from their daily lives on tomb walls, they left little information about their mummification practices. A mummy now in Hildesheim, Germany, has some pictures of embalming on its case, but they do not tell us the full story. The most detailed information we have is from a Greek writer named Herodotus (c. 485–425 BC). When he visited Egypt during the fifth century BC he wrote down what the priests told him about mummifying bodies. They said the process took 70 days to complete. In modern times people have done experiments to determine how long it takes to mummify a body. They have found out that it takes 40 days to dry out a body, and this was probably the time it took in ancient Egypt.

Fashions in mummy-making

After 40 days the body was washed, dried, and rubbed with oils to make the skin more supple. Often during this period the internal organs that had been removed were covered with natron and wrapped in linen. Then they were put back in the chest and stomach areas of the body. There were different fashions in embalming and sometimes the organs were put in canopic jars. Often a **plaque** was put over the embalming cut in the abdomen to stop evil spirits from entering the mummy. There was another fashion that started in the 21st Dynasty. After the pile of natron salt was removed the body always looked **emaciated** because all the moisture had been removed. So the embalmers would push sawdust or linen strips under the top layer of skin to make the body look plumper. They would also place false eyes made from colored stone over the eyelids to make the face look more lifelike.

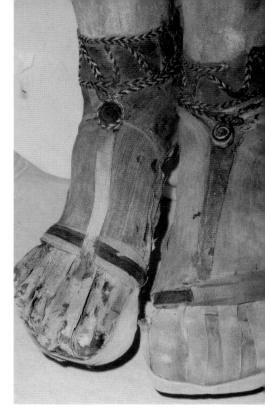

The feet of a mummy, wrapped in linen. The embalmers have made some pretend sandals from linen.

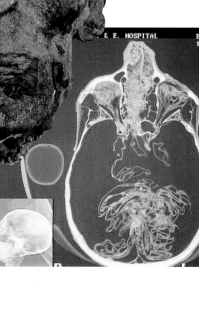

After the brain was taken out, the head of this mummy (left) was packed with strips of linen. The linen strips are the wavy white lines in the X-ray film below.

The all-important beetle

The body was then wrapped in many layers of linen strips. The embalmers placed jewelry and **amulets** between the linen layers to protect the mummy. Sometimes a stone carved in the shape of a **scarab beetle** was placed on the chest, near the heart. An inscription written on the flat base of the **heart scarab** said that the dead man or woman had been a good person and would like to enter the afterlife. The heart scarab was useful for the dead person when they were judged by the gods, in case the embalmers had accidentally pulled out the heart or if the heart had decayed. When the wrapping was finished the embalmers put more jewelry on the mummy and perhaps placed a mask over the head and shoulders. Black **resin** was poured over some mummies, making the outer layer of linen hard and strong. Now the mummy was ready to be put into a coffin and then into its final resting place, the tomb.

A finished mummy in an anthropoid coffin. "Anthropoid" means shaped like a person.

Who was mummified in ancient Egypt? Our information from the writer Herodotus shows that there were three grades of mummy-making, each with a different price. Even the lowest price was too expensive for ordinary people, so clearly mummification was only for the wealthy: priests and priestesses, nobles and, of course, the king and his family. We know our mummy Hornedjitef was a high-ranking priest so we would expect his body to be mummified to the highest standard. Later, we will investigate whether this was true or not!

Mummy surprises

When a mummy is examined, sometimes there are surprises. Occasionally, some parts of the body are missing, maybe an arm or a leg. This probably happened as bodies waiting to be mummified began to decay and fall apart. In a few mummies these missing limbs are replaced by sticks of wood. In other mummies, for some reason, the ancient embalmers included extra limbs or skulls within the mummy package!

A mummified young baboon. Some of the linen wrappings have fallen off, showing the animal's fur beneath.

The Egyptians didn't only mummify people. When they entered the afterlife they expected to see again everything they had seen in this life, particularly their animals. So a whole variety of creatures were mummified: birds, reptiles, fish and mammals, such as cats, dogs, and baboons. Visitors to temples in the **Ptolemaic** (and later **Roman**) **periods** could buy an animal to offer it to a particular god.

3 How do we know about Hornedjitef, and other mummies?

T he mummies we see in museums today originally came from tombs in Egypt. Many hundreds of mummies have already been found, and many more are likely to be found as **archaeologists** look for them on archaeological **excavations**. It is important for us to think about how mummies were treated years ago and what happens to them now.

A modern-archaeologist carefully uncovers an ancient body at an excavation in the Delta area of Egypt.

We are always curious about what happened hundreds of years ago. Ideally, on an archaeological excavation all information should be recorded. Unfortunately, on some excavations done during the 19th and early 20th centuries not everything was recorded properly, and this was particularly so for mummies. In some cases useful information was recorded but was later lost. For many mummies we do not know exactly where in Egypt they came from, often because nobody bothered to write down the information. Fortunately, this wasn't always the case. Two archaeologists who worked in Egypt are particularly famous for the amount of detailed information they wrote down about the things they found on their excavations.

The beautifully decorated mummy of a young man named Artemidorus was given to the British Museum in 1888. Flinders Petrie found this mummy in a place named Hawara, to the west of modern Cairo.

In this 1922 photograph, the British Egyptologist Sir Matthew Flinders Petrie is striding through the Egyptian desert at a place named Abydos.

The mummy of a young woman named Hermione. You can see her name written on the right-hand side of her portrait. Beneath her name is the word "grammatike." Once people thought this meant she was a school teacher. Now we think it means she knew how to read and write.

Flinders Petrie

Flinders Petrie (1852–1942) is known as the father of British **Egyptology**. He thought it was very important to record all things found on an excavation. Flinders Petrie lived and worked in Egypt for a long time and was responsible for finding hundreds of mummies and other objects. At the time when the Romans ruled Egypt many of the mummies had a portrait of the dead person put in the wrappings. Petrie found hundreds of these portrait mummies, and two of them are particularly interesting as they have the dead person's name written on them. The mummy of Artemidorus is in a reddish-brown case covered with beautiful gold decoration, and he can now be seen in the British Museum. The mummy of Hermione is now in Girton College, Cambridge, and her linen wrappings are in a diamond-shaped design. Both of these mummies have Greek names, like the kings who ruled Egypt when Hornedjitef was alive, but the actual people lived several centuries after him.

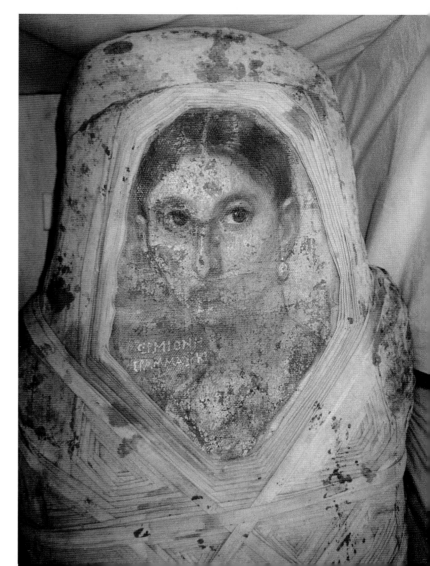

The author, Joyce Filer, examining one of Tutankhamun's gold coffins in the young king's tomb in the Valley of the Kings.

This photograph of Howard Carter was taken as he worked in the tomb of Tutankhamun in the 1920s. Howard Carter is the man on the left.

Tutankhamun

When he was learning about archaeology, Howard Carter (1874–1939) worked with Flinders Petrie and probably learned to make detailed records from him. Howard Carter is famous for finding the tomb and mummy of Tutankhamun (c. 1333–1323 BC), a young king who lived during the 18th Dynasty. In 1922, after working for many years in Egypt, Carter found the tomb, which had been accidentally covered over by the stone chippings from the building of another tomb nearby. Tutankhamun's tomb was packed with hundreds of items that had been buried with him, including **shrines**, furniture, chariots, jewelry, and

statues. Then of course, most important, there was the mummy of the king himself. Howard Carter and Dr. Derry, an English doctor working in Cairo, examined the mummy of Tutankhamun. They found out that he was about 18 years old when he died and that, even though he had been properly mummified, the skin on the mummy was in very poor condition. Not many people know that there were actually three mummies in Tutankhamun's tomb! The mummified bodies of two babies were also in the tomb. Carter and Derry examined them. They found out that the mummies were both girls and that one of them would have been disabled had she lived. Many people would like to think that these were the daughters of Tutankhamun but so far it is not known if they were related to the king. There were so many objects in the tomb that it took Carter ten years to write down all the information about the objects he found. It is thanks to his notes that we know so much about this young king.

Strange goings-on

Europeans have been interested in Egypt and mummies for quite a long time. The English playwright William Shakespeare mentions mummies in some of his plays and, of course, he wrote the famous play *Antony and Cleopatra*. In the 17th century, Samuel Pepys mentions in one of his diaries that he saw Egyptian mummies in a warehouse.

A scene from an old black-and-white film telling the story of Antony and Cleopatra, the famous Egyptian queen.

A poster from 1842 advertising some mummies on show in Bath, England. It cost about seven cents to see the mummies.

English tourists visiting the Giza pyramids in 1899.

Europeans and Americans are among those who have done strange and destructive things with mummies. For example, in the 16th century, King François I of France (1515–47) believed that Egyptian mummies had magical powers and eating them would cure illnesses, so he always traveled with a bag of crushed mummy powder and rhubarb. Powdered mummy has also been used to make brown paint for artists. An American paper factory owner used linen mummy wrappings to make brown paper, and when coal was too expensive to buy for the Egyptian steam railways mummies were burnt as fuel! Thousands of mummies have already been destroyed.

Souvenirs

In the 19th century many Europeans traveled around Egypt and brought back mummies as souvenirs. These were often sold in auctions in Europe and the United States. If it was too difficult to travel with a whole mummy then often heads, hands, or feet would be snapped off and kept. There was such a demand for mummies that local Egyptians would make fake ones to sell to European tourists. Today, most tourists are more interested in learning about ancient Egypt than collecting bits of mummies.

The right hand from a mummy. Mummy hands were often snapped off because people were interested in the rings on the fingers.

Unwrapping mummies

Europeans were very curious about how mummies were made and why they lasted so long without decaying. Until recently there was no way of examining the inside of a mummy without taking it apart. Often these unwrappings (or unrollings as they were sometimes known) were social occasions. Many mummies were destroyed by unwrapping them. Only on a few occasions were these mummy unwrappings done scientifically, with the person doing the unwrapping writing down what he saw. In 1825 Dr. Augustus Granville, a doctor to Queen Victoria's family, wrote about a female mummy (and coffin) he had bought from an American for four dollars. He unwrapped the mummy before an audience and gave away pieces of the mummy to members of the audience, but he kept some for himself. These he labeled and then put in a specially-made box. It is likely that many mummies were destroyed in this way.

The author explains the mysteries of Egyptian tombs to two young companions, Verity and Guy.

Before X rays were discovered, mummies were unwrapped to find out their secrets. In this 19th-century painting a group of French Egyptologists are taking a mummy apart.

The mummy of Hornedjitef in its decorated cartonnage cover, lying in the bottom half of the inner coffin. (You can read more about the coffin on pages 40–43).

After excavating an ancient Egyptian body in northern Egypt, the author records important details, such as its condition, measurements, and the grave goods in the tomb.

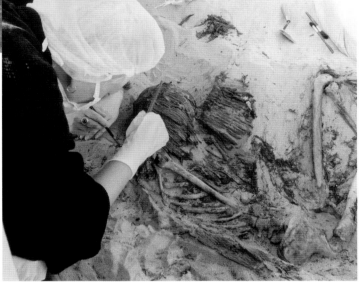

Archaeologists carefully brushing a sand-dried body covered with a reed mat.

X rays

These days we have a different attitude toward mummies. We want to know about them but we do not need to destroy them in order to find out about them. We can use different types of X rays to examine them. The mummy of Hornedjitef was studied in this way. Scholars also have an improved attitude toward mummies found on archaeological excavations. Wherever they are found, in tombs or in the ground, it is important that all information is recorded in different ways. Once things are moved it is very difficult to rely only on memory.

Recording the details

How might a mummy or skeleton be recorded on an excavation? As soon as a mummy is found it should be photographed, and possibly drawn, before anything else is done. Then any sand and stones around the mummy are cleared away carefully, using either a trowel or a brush. When the mummy can be clearly seen it should be measured and photographed again. The mummy is then brushed carefully to remove dust and dirt. Then details of the condition of the mummy, its measurements and decorations, are recorded. Only after all this has been done can the mummy be carefully moved into a storehouse. Some archaeological groups working in Egypt have their own portable X-ray machine to examine mummies.

4 Finding clues to Hornedjitef's home and family life

When Hornedjitef grew up he became a priest in a temple in Thebes. What was his life like before he became a priest? When Hornedjitef was alive the Greeks ruled Egypt. Thebes was the Greek name for the ancient town the Egyptians called Waset. Thebes had been an important town in Egypt for a long time and many rulers chose it as their capital.

A modern Egyptian boy carrying bundles of reeds on his donkey.

The river and the desert

Thebes was built around the Nile River, which at 4,350 miles is the world's longest river. The Nile had a great influence on how the people of Egypt lived. Every year the river would flood its banks, spreading a thick layer of fine soil called silt across the fields. This silt was so rich it was almost black. This caused the Egyptians to call their land Kemet, or the "Black Land." Farmers dug channels in their fields to bring the water from the river and then they planted crops in the fertile silt and waited for them to grow. If in some years the river flooded too much then the crops would drown, and if in other years there was not enough water the crops could not begin to grow.

The Nile River was also the country's source of water for drinking and washing, as well as a means of travel. Boats made of bundles of **papyrus** or light wood, with linen sails, would go up and down the Nile collecting and delivering food and other goods, including mummies going to their funerals.

Next to the fertile strips of land were large areas of dry desert where nothing would grow, so the Egyptians buried their dead there. On the west bank of the Nile opposite Thebes there are large areas of rock formations where tombs were built. The Egyptians were nervous about the desert, especially at night, because they knew wild animals, such as jackals lived there.

Farmers dug channels, or ditches, in the fields to allow water to travel to their crops.

The ancient Egyptians feared jackals like this one but they also admired the animal's cleverness. They associated jackals with Anubis, the god of embalming.

Egyptian houses today are similar to those from ancient times.

Daily life

As the young Hornedjitef walked around Thebes he must have seen people getting on with their daily life. He saw the farmers working in the fields growing fruit, vegetables, and grain for making into bread. An important job was looking after the animals—sheep, goats, and cattle. These animals provided the Egyptians with milk, meat, and skins for making leather. They also got meat and eggs from birds, such as ducks, geese, pigeons, and chickens.

Tomb paintings show how important cattle were to the ancient Egyptians.

Hornedjitef's home

Hornedjitef's family was probably fairly wealthy. He has left us no information about his family but they probably lived in a house similar to those seen in Egypt today. It would have been one or more stories high, built of bricks made from mud. The windows would have been small to keep out the heat and flies. Like today, people spent a lot of time outside. His family might have had a garden with a pond stocked with fish, and some trees to provide shade.

Hornedjitef's house may have had a garden with a pond surrounded by fruit trees, like this one from a New Kingdom tomb painting.

As he passed different workshops Hornedjitef saw meat being prepared and bakers making bread in hot ovens. Bread was the main part of everybody's meal and was made in the same way as it is in Egypt today. Loaves of partly-baked bread were also put into large jars with water to **ferment** and make beer.

A modern Egyptian woman baking bread in a cone-shaped oven, just as people did thousands of years ago.

Cool clothes

Like other ancient
Egyptians, Hornedjitef wore
simple clothing made out of
linen, which helped to keep him
cool. The Egyptians grew fields of
flax. This provided thread that could be
spun and woven into linen for clothing,
bedsheets and, of course, wrappings for
mummies. Many Egyptians walked barefoot
but Hornedjitef would have protected his feet
by wearing thonged sandals, rather like modern
flip-flops, made from papyrus.

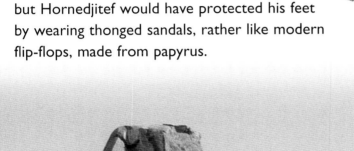

*Hornedjitef may
have worn papyrus
sandals like
these.*

Ancient monuments

It is important to remember that when Hornedjitef
was a boy living in Thebes some of the **monuments**
that we think of as ancient were already old! Like us,
he too would have walked by the Colossi of Memnon
and he may even have visited the pyramids and the
Sphinx at Giza, perhaps with his father.

*The Colossi of Memnon are
two huge statues standing
about 59 feet tall. They were
already hundreds of years
old by the time Hornedjitef
was born.*

A tomb painting showing servants carrying a gazelle, some hares, and bundles of cereals.

Hornedjitef's family

As he was growing up, the two most important things in Hornedjitef's life were his family and his education. We do not know how many people there were in his family, or how many brothers and sisters he had, but we do know that families in ancient Egypt could be quite large. His father was head of the household and made all the important family decisions. It is possible that his father was also a priest. His mother was in charge of running the house and because his family was wealthy they would have had servants to help her with the work. Like people today Hornedjitef may have had a pet dog, or a cat similar to those we see in Egyptian paintings and statues.

Hornedjitef may have had a pet cat like this one, which is identical in color to cats seen in Egyptian tomb paintings.

Going to school

In ancient Egypt most people could not read and write. Those who could were able to get good jobs as scribes. People would pay scribes to write their letters for them. A scribe could earn a good living working for wealthy landowners, recording numbers of cattle and how much food was produced. Hornedjitef was taught to read and write either at school or by a tutor at home. Surprisingly, we do not have much information from ancient Egypt about actual schools. We do know that groups of boys practiced writing stories and reading aloud and that they learned arithmetic. They wrote with a brush and ink on wooden boards covered with **gesso**. Any mistakes on these could be easily wiped out. Although Hornedjitef does not tell us anything about his education, we can look at the words of another high priest of Amun at Karnak, Bek-enkhons. He lived much earlier than Hornedjitef, during the reign of the king Ramesses II (1290–1224 BC). Some writing on a statue of Beken-khons tells us that he spent four years in an elementary school in a temple at Karnak. Then he learned to be an administrator and this took him another 11 years. After that he went on to become a priest.

The writing on this statue of the priest Bekenkhons tells us about the education of wealthy young men in ancient Egypt.

We do not know how long Hornedjitef's education took. He obviously learned useful things because, like Bekenkhons, he went on to become a high-level priest at Karnak.

5 What was Egypt like when Hornedjitef was alive?

When Hornedjitef was alive, the Greeks ruled Egypt. The Greeks did not call their rulers Pharaoh like the Egyptians, they called them kings. The king at this time was called Ptolemy III. He ruled from 246 to 222 BC. But how did a Greek family come to reign in Egypt?

At various times during Egypt's history when there wasn't a strong ruler, the country was taken over by foreigners. In 332 BC a Greek king named Alexander (356–323 BC) conquered Egypt when he was only 20 years old. But this was not the first time that foreigners had taken over Egypt. When Alexander arrived, people from Persia (modern Iran) were already ruling Egypt. The Persians had invaded and conquered the country in 343 BC. Alexander planned a new capital city on the northern coast of Egypt in the **Delta** area. Although he did not live long enough to see the city finished it was named after him. Alexandria continued to be the capital of Egypt during the years that the Greeks ruled Egypt.

The Ptolemies

After Alexander died in 323 BC one of his generals took control of Egypt. His name was Ptolemy (c. 305–285 BC) and his **descendants** ruled Egypt for 300 years. This is known as the Ptolemaic period. Ptolemy I continued building the city of Alexandria and made it an important cultural center. He ordered his architects to build the Pharos lighthouse, one of the seven wonders of the ancient world, and the Alexandria library. This library was the greatest in the classical world, but it burned down during a war between Egypt and Rome in 30 BC. Recently, underwater archaeologists have been working in the Mediterranean Sea looking for buildings and statues that fell into the sea from Alexandria.

Coins showing portraits of Ptolemy III and his wife, Berenice.

Hornedjitef lived during the reign of Ptolemy III. Ptolemy's second name was Euergetes, which means "benefactor," so he is often known as Ptolemy III Euergetes. Ptolemy's wife was Berenice II. They had six children. We have some idea of what Ptolemy III, Queen Berenice II, and their son looked like from their statues and from their images on coins.

An underwater archaeologist working on the sea bed near Alexandria.

Speaking and writing

The new Greek rulers respected the cultures and traditions of the Egyptians and for the ordinary person life carried on in the usual way. The new rulers, however, spoke Greek and this was the official language under the Ptolemaic kings. It is possible that many of the rulers did not even speak the Egyptian language. The most famous member of the Ptolemaic rulers, Queen Cleopatra (51–30 BC), was different. She could speak Egyptian, her own Greek language, and several other languages as well. By this time, hieroglyphs were only used for religious inscriptions and the priests used a script called demotic for ordinary writing. As the people living in Egypt at this time understood different languages we sometimes see the same important information from the king written in more than one language. The Rosetta Stone, now in the British Museum, is a good example of this. Written in 196 BC (after the time of Ptolemy III and Hornedjitef) it has a **decree** from Ptolemy V on it. The message is written in two languages, Egyptian and Greek, and in three scripts—two types of Egyptian writing and the Greek alphabet.

Queen Cleopatra and her son Caesarion.

The Rosetta Stone. The same message is written in the Greek language and in the Egyptian language.

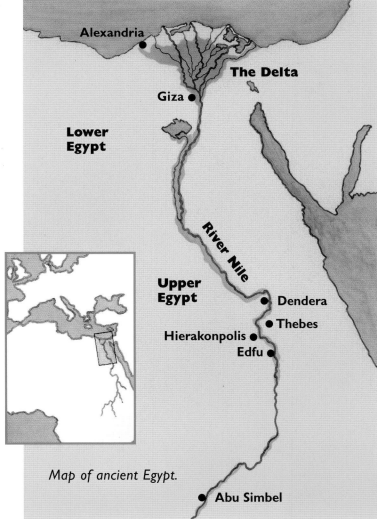

Map of ancient Egypt.

Records—and riots

We know a good deal about life under the Ptolemaic kings because of the large number of papyrus scrolls that have been found in Egypt, many of them written in Greek. The Ptolemaic kings were very good at administration, and at keeping written records. Some of the scrolls that have been found are letters, some are lists. Others tell us about the laws in Egypt at this time and what people bought and sold. These scrolls also tell us of some of the problems that upset the Egyptian people. At one time under Ptolemy III the people were fed up with paying taxes (just like today!). They complained and rioted. Other scrolls show that the native Egyptians were not always on friendly terms with the Greeks who came to live in Egypt. Some Egyptians felt that the Greeks were treated better than they were.

There were many different peoples living in Egypt at this time. In the streets of the cities you could see Egyptians, Greeks, Persians, and Nubians. Sometimes these different peoples intermarried and had children.

Measurements were taken from two skulls from unwrapped mummies to make these model heads. Left: a bronze model of a middle-aged man. Right: a wax model of a woman. Both lived in Egypt during the Greco-Roman period.

A Nubian man.

The riches of the world

Before the Greek period in Egypt few people used money. Usually people bartered items such as food, pottery, and clothing for other things that they needed. In Ptolemaic times, silver and gold coins were used to buy these goods.

Rome

Greece

Sicily

Crete

Lebanon

Libya

EGYPT

Nubia

Map showing the different countries with which the Egyptians traded.

24

Like the other Ptolemaic kings, Ptolemy III was interested in trading with other countries. Egypt exported papyrus, linen, and grain to exchange for items people needed and could not produce themselves. So traders traveled south into Nubia trading for gold, heavy woods like ebony for building, exotic animals like big cats and giraffes, ivory, and spices. They went north to different parts of the Mediterranean area, exchanging their goods for cedar wood from Lebanon, olive oil from Crete, and silver from Syria. They also traveled east to Arabia looking for incense and other exotic goods. Today **papyrus** grows in Palermo, Sicily, because Greek traders took it there.

A tomb painting showing Nubians carrying gold and foodstuffs. Notice the man on the right is carrying the skin of a big cat.

Persia (Iran)

Arabia

Troubles

In the ancient world during the time of Ptolemy III Egypt was quite a strong and wealthy country. Occasionally wars broke out and if Egypt felt threatened, then Ptolemy III would send his army to fight. When soldiers returned to Egypt after fighting Ptolemy III gave them land in return for their service. The soldiers built houses on this land for themselves and their families.

Evidence from mummies and skeletons tells us that people in Hornedjitef's time became sick just as they do today. People suffered from headaches, toothaches, and back problems. Sometimes people broke their arms and legs, or suffered serious diseases like leprosy or tuberculosis. In the ancient world people thought that Egyptian doctors were very good, and it is possible that there were doctors to look after particular parts of the body. Wealthy people paid doctors to try and cure them, but poor people had to help themselves. As well as taking herbal medicines, both rich and poor people used magic spells to help them get better.

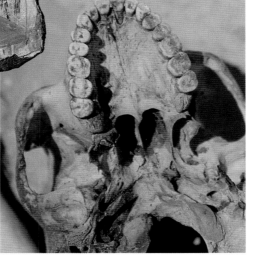

Many ancient Egyptians had badly worn teeth like this. Some had painful abscesses (tooth infections).

Many ancient Egyptians had backaches caused by arthritis. The wavy edges on these bones in the spine show damage caused by arthritis.

6 A servant of the god

The god Anubis and the god Thoth.

Religion was a very important part of ancient Egyptian life. There were more than seven hundred gods and goddesses. The Egyptians believed that there was a god to look after every event or problem in life. The most important gods and goddesses had their own temples, where groups of priests and priestesses worked for the god. People believed that the temple was the home of the god. Many of the gods and goddesses had particular animals associated with them. Thoth, the god of learning and writing, was associated with the ibis bird and with baboons. Cats were the animals associated with Bastet, a protective goddess. Anubis, the god of embalming, was associated with the jackal. Some of these animals, such as cats and ibises, lived in the temple and were looked after by servants. Many of these animals representing a god were mummified and buried in tombs when they died.

A statue of Horus as a falcon from the temple at Edfu.

The massive entrance to the temple at Edfu. You can see the two large falcon statues on either side of the gateway.

Temples

We can still see many temples from different periods in Egyptian history, for example Luxor Temple, begun in the time of Amenhotep III (1390–1352 BC), the Ramesseum, built by Ramesses II (1279–1213 BC) and Medinet Habu, built by Ramesses III (1184–1153 BC).

There are several surviving temples from the Ptolemaic period. The Ptolemaic kings spent a great deal of money building them, and they have lasted well. Of all the temples in Egypt, the best preserved is at Edfu in **Upper Egypt**. It is the Temple of Horus, who has the falcon as his special creature. The temple at Edfu is one of the largest in Egypt and is decorated with carvings showing the feasts and festivals that happened in the temple every year. Two big, beautifully carved statues of Horus as a falcon stand at the entrance. The Temple of Dendera is in Upper Egypt and belonged to the goddess Hathor. Hathor was the goddess of love and beauty, and her associated animal was the cow. Other famous temples dating to Ptolemaic times are at Esna, Philae, and Kom Ombo.

The Temple of Amun

The most important temple in this story is the Temple of Amun at Karnak, where Hornedjitef worked as a priest. Amun was the most important god of ancient Egypt. His associated animals were the ram and the goose. His name meant "The Hidden One." Statues of Amun or pictures of him on temple walls show him wearing two tall feathers on his head and a false beard. Ptolemy III built a beautifully decorated gate to honor the god near one of the temples at Karnak.

Although Hornedjitef worked in the Temple of Amun, he was no ordinary priest. The many titles on his funerary papyrus and coffin suggest that he was a very high-ranking priest. It is possible that he was so high up in his profession that lesser priests thought he had special powers. How did he get to such a high position?

A large decorated gate at the Temple of Karnak. It was built by King Ptolemy III Euergetes.

Part of the Temple of Amun at Karnak, showing the sacred lake.

The ram was one of the creatures associated with the chief of gods, Amun.

27

This photograph shows how massive the Karnak temple area really is!

Statue of a young priest. He has a shaved head and wears a short linen kilt.

Training to be a priest

As a child Hornedjitef was taught to read and write, just like other boys who hoped to be scribes or priests. Hornedjitef has not left us any information about how he trained to be a priest, but our friend the priest Bekenkhons does tell us about his training. After 15 years of education Bekenkhons went to work as a priest in the Temple of Amun at Karnak. He started as a low-level priest, and it seems he was told what to do by his father, who also worked in the temple. Bekenkhons stayed at this level for four years, and then little by little he was given promotion. The inscription on his statue tells us that after

39 years he became high priest, and he worked at this high-level job for 27 years. After all this work Bekenkhons must have been quite an old man when he died! Hornedjitef probably also had to work his way up to the top.

Serving the gods

What did priests and priestesses actually do in ancient Egypt? Religious scenes on temple walls show only the ruling king standing with and serving the gods. This is because the ancient Egyptians believed that only the king was special enough to talk directly to the gods. In real life, however, it was priests like Hornedjitef who served the gods. The ancient Egyptian word for priest means "god's servant" so the priests had to look after the statue of the god or goddess of a particular temple. The statue of the god was kept in a **shrine**.

Priests at work

There were different ranks or levels of priest, each doing a different job. Priests were paid for their work, according to the importance of their particular job. The lector-priests read and made copies of sacred books. *Ka* priests served the *ka*, or spirit of mummies. Other priests called the "hour priests" decided when it was the right time to hold a festival or a service. They did this by carefully watching the movements of the moon and stars to tell them the time. Other priests carried the closed shrine after the god's statue had been taken out. Some priests and priestesses were singers and made music during festivals and services in the temple.

As a "god's servant" or high priest, Hornedjitef was one of the few people allowed to touch the statue of Amun, the god of his temple. Hornedjitef would open the shrine and take out the statue of Amun. Then he would close the shrine and tell a lower-level priest to carry it around the temple during festivals.

Statue of Sematawy, an older priest. He has a shaved head, and he is holding a sacred shrine.

Hornedjitef would put robes on the statue and present it with food. With other high-ranking priests he would then carry Amun's statue around the temple area.

Priests were also involved in funerals. A priest led the procession of mourners in a funeral. He would also offer prayers to the gods as the mummy was taken to its tomb.

This scene from a papyrus shows people at a funeral. The dead man has been mummified and is waiting to be taken to his tomb. His wife kneels beside him, crying. Mourners in a procession follow behind.

Other duties

Animals were highly prized in ancient Egypt and so cattle were usually only killed on special occasions. The animals were killed quickly in an **abattoir** and the pieces of meat were presented to the gods during festivals. One of Hornedjitef's titles says that he was "overseer of the abattoir" but this does not mean that he killed animals. He was in charge of checking that the meat was kept clean and used properly in religious ceremonies.

Another of Hornedjitef's titles says that he was a "follower of the queen." We know that some of the Ptolemaic queens were worshipped as goddesses when they died. Queen Arsinoe II, step-mother to Ptolemy III, was made into a goddess after her death and it is possible that Hornedjitef was also one of her priests as well as being a priest of Amun.

Limestone statue of Queen Arsinoe II. Hornedjitef may have been one of her special priests when she was made into a goddess.

Festivals and funerals

Throughout Egypt the priests and priestesses held many festivals to honor the large number of gods and goddesses. The more important gods and goddesses had the most festivals. In the Temple of Ptah at Memphis a specially picked black bull with a white star on its brow was treated like a god. The priests at Memphis often held processions in honor of the Apis bull, thought to be Ptah's living image. The bull had his own servants and when he died he was mummified and given a special funeral. Then the priests had to search Egypt for another identical bull. This routine went on for hundreds of years and was particularly important during the Ptolemaic period.

Bronze statue of a priest named Khonsuirdas. You can see that Khonsuirdas is wearing the skin of a big cat, which means he was a very important priest like Hornedjitef.

Statue of an Apis bull. These bulls were very special and were looked after carefully.

37449

The great gateway of the Temple of Luxor.

One of the most important festivals at Thebes was the Festival of Opet, in honor of the god Osiris. Here the statues of the different gods from the different temples at Karnak were taken up the river on boats to the Temple of Luxor. The king and his family would watch the processions of people laughing, singing, and dancing as they followed the statues.

Washing, wigs, and wives

As a priest Hornedjitef had to shave all the hair from his head and body—the Egyptians believed hair on priests was unclean. Priests sometimes wore wigs. Before Hornedjitef entered the temple he had to wash himself. Priests had to be clean before they went into the temple. The Greek writer Herodotus tells us that priests were not allowed to wear woolen clothing—wool was also thought to be unclean. Hornedjitef wore linen clothes like the other priests. High-status priests wore the skins from exotic cats like leopards or cheetahs, and Hornedjitef may have done the same.

Priests could get married and it is likely that Hornedjitef had a wife and family somewhere in Thebes. After they died his wife and children would have been mummified, but we do not know where to find their mummies.

This strange-looking object is actually a man's wig. Priests shaved their head but they could wear a wig like this when they were not inside a temple.

It is very likely that Hornedjitef was married and had children. This is the mummy of the wife of a priest who lived in Egypt during the Roman period.

31

7 The mummy speaks

Mummies were often taken from Egypt and sold in Europe and the United States. Some were destroyed when they were unwrapped. Today experts do not need to take mummies apart in order to find out about them because we have scientific techniques to help us. X rays are used to help living people but can also be used safely on mummies. Although X rays were discovered at the end of the 19th century they were not regularly used to examine mummies until much later. X rays have proved to be very useful in showing us what is inside mummy packages. The great archaeologist Flinders Petrie was one of the first people to realize this.

What X rays can tell us

There are important questions to ask about any mummy. How much of the body is inside the package? Is the body that of a man or a woman, or a boy or girl? How old was the person when he or she died? Can we find out about any illnesses or health problems they had when they were alive? What can we find out about making mummies in ancient Egypt? X rays can help us find out the answers.

However, there are some problems with ordinary X-ray machines. One problem is that both sides of a mummy are seen on an X-ray film at the same time. This sometimes makes it difficult to "read" the X rays. Another problem is that ordinary X rays cannot see through very thick layers of linen or layers of **resin** covering a body. This was one of the problems when Hornedjitef was first X rayed in the 1960s. These X rays showed that there was a human body inside the mummy, but not all details could be seen clearly. The X rays could not see into his head because of the thick layers of linen and resin. Full information about Hornedjitef remained a mystery until his mummy was examined again in the 1990s using a newer and more powerful type of machine.

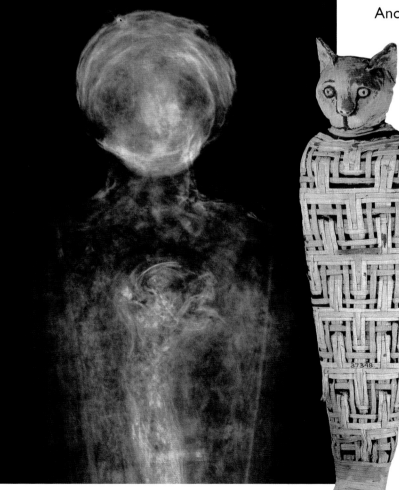

For a long time nobody knew if there was a cat's body inside this mummy. It certainly looks like a cat from the outside! X rays showed that there were two cats, not one, inside. The X ray shows the skull of an adult cat at the top and the body of a little kitten in the middle part of the mummy. Why the ancient Egyptians did this will remain a mystery.

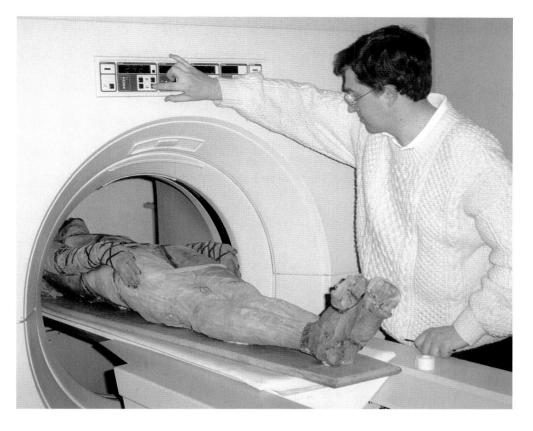

This radiographer, Paul Smith, is specially trained to use a CAT scanning machine. The machine can tell us what is inside this mummy. You have already seen the beautifully wrapped feet of the same mummy on page 10.

British Museum staff Darrel Day, Bob Dominey, and John Hayman carefully carry Hornedjitef, packed in a crate, down to a van waiting outside the British Museum.

The CAT scanner

In 1973 hospitals started using a new type of X-ray machine called a **CAT scanner**. A computer is used to record and keep the information. It was quickly realized that this machine was powerful enough to see through the thick layers of linen and resin that had caused problems for ordinary X-ray machines. Over the years dozens of other mummies in different museums in the world have been examined using a CAT scanner. So it seemed the ideal way to find out more about the secrets of Hornedjitef.

Hornedjitef visits a hospital

One evening in 1995, Hornedjitef was carefully packed into a crate, loaded into a van, and taken to Princess Grace Hospital in London. The beautifully decorated gold cover on the mummy is fragile and might have been damaged, so it was removed and kept safely in the British Museum.

At the hospital the mummy of Hornedjitef was unpacked from his crate and laid on the table section of the scanning machine. When the doctors and nurses at the hospital saw the mummy they were very excited because they had never been so close to an ancient Egyptian mummy before! Like the people in the 19th century they too wanted to see what was inside the mummy, but this time the mummy being examined would not be harmed.

Into the scanner

The CAT scanner is a massive machine with a circular hole in the middle. The table with the mummy passes through this hole so that X-ray pictures can be taken, and the height of the table can be changed by moving it up and down. It also moves in and out of the scanning machine. It is dangerous to be in the same room when the scanner is working because there is harmful radiation, so the radiographer who works the machine sits in a separate room.

The table moved Hornedjitef in and out of the machine a little bit at a time. Every time the table was moved an X-ray picture was taken of his body. Each of these pictures is called a "slice" but the mummy was not sliced or cut in any way. These slices can be put together by a computer to make a three-dimensional image. You can see some three-dimensional scans of Hornedjitef on pages 38–39.

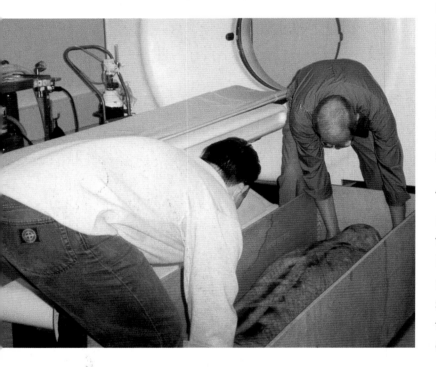

It is important to handle mummies very carefully. Hornedjitef is taken from the crate and placed on the CAT scanning table in the hospital.

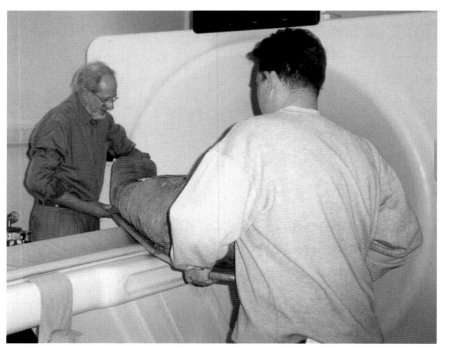

The examination of Hornedjitef took several hours. The radiographers took 246 X-ray pictures that were recorded on the computer. These would be looked at to answer important questions about the life of this priest.

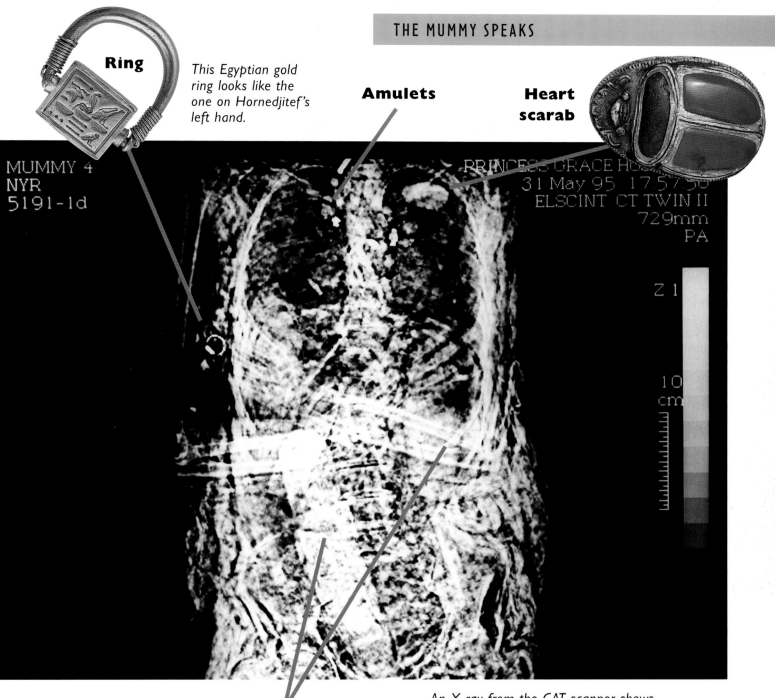

Ring

This Egyptian gold ring looks like the one on Hornedjitef's left hand.

Amulets

Heart scarab

MUMMY 4
NYR
5191-1d

PRINCESS GRACE HO...
31 May 95 17.57...
ELSCINT CT TWIN II
729mm
PA

Z 1

10
cm

Packages

An X ray from the CAT scanner shows Hornedjitef's arms folded across his chest. He is wearing a ring on his left hand and there are packages inside the body. Near his left shoulder (at the top of the X ray) you can see a heart scarab. It seems to have slipped from its proper place on Hornedjitef's chest.

Was he all there?

So what did the CAT scanner tell us about Hornedjitef? Obviously, it was not surprising to find out that there was a human body inside the linen wrappings because scholars already knew that from the X-ray examination in the 1960s. We did want to know how much of the body was there. This may seem a strange question but remember that sometimes the ancient embalmers lost parts of bodies or even added extra bits into mummy packages! The CAT scanner showed that none of Hornedjitef's body was missing—it was all there, except for some teeth.

35

A man or a woman?

Although this mummy has a man's name no one could be sure that there was a man's body inside—again, this is not silly. There have been a few mistaken identities in ancient Egyptian mummies! Scientists can tell from the bones of a skeleton if the person was a man or a woman. Men's bones are usually a lot stronger, longer, and heavier than women's bones. There are important differences between men and women's skull and hip bones.

Man

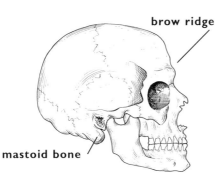

Woman

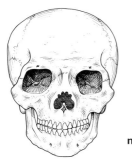

These drawings show the places where a man's skull differs from a woman's.

Parts of the skull, such as the brow ridges and the hard bone behind the ears called the mastoid bone, are usually much bigger in men. Men often have larger, square **jaws** while women have smaller and more pointed jaws. The really important differences between men and women are seen in the **pelvic bones**. Women's hips are much wider and roomier than men's. This is so that there is enough room for a baby to grow. Men's hips are narrower.

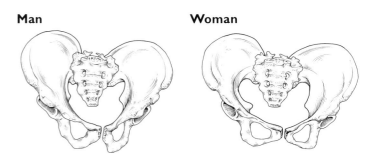

A woman's hip bones have a different shape to a man's hip bones.

The evidence from the CAT scans shows us that the bones in the Hornedjitef mummy are large and strong. The skull has large brow ridges and mastoid bones and is large and strong at the back. The jaw is large and square. This information, together with the shape of the hip bones, tell us that this is the body of a man, which matches the male name for the mummy.

The decorated gold mask, which covers Hornedjitef's head. The face looks young, but how old was he when he died?

What age?

Looking at Hornedjitef's **funerary mask**, the face looks fairly young. Was Hornedjitef really young when he died? It was not unusual for an ancient Egyptian funerary mask to be made to look like a young person even if the dead person wearing it was elderly. This was because the ancient Egyptians believed that people would become young again in the afterlife. So how can a person's age at death be discovered by studying a skeleton? Experts look at the bones and teeth to see how far they have grown. For example, on X rays of a young person's long bones—their arms and legs—there are little caps of bone separated from the main bone. An elastic tissue called cartilage grows between them. As a person grows this cartilage changes into bone. Then more and more cartilage is produced, which is also changed into bone. The bone is built up in layers, and when a person has finished growing the separate caps fix onto the bone.

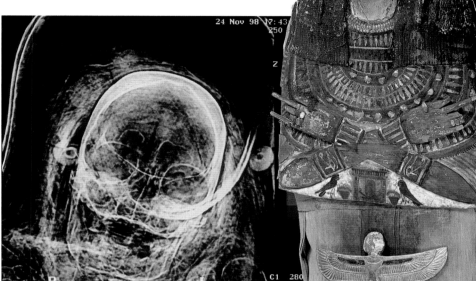

Right: the mask on this mummy of a woman named Katebet suggests she was a young woman, but the CAT scan (below) tells us that she was elderly when she died. You can see she has lost nearly all her teeth.

24 Nov 98 17:43
250

Part of the skeleton of a young person. You can see a separate cap of bone at the top of the left arm bone. This means that the person was not a fully grown adult.

The scans show very clearly that Hornedjitef was an adult when he died. As the bones of a skeleton grow and develop so do the teeth. A young person has a first set of teeth, which are sometimes known as baby teeth. These gradually fall out and are replaced by adult teeth. In ancient Egypt there was lots of sand and grit in food. This wore down teeth more and more as people grew older. Looking at teeth to see how worn they are is a good way to assess the person's age at death. Throughout life people lose teeth, either through accident or disease. Hornedjitef had lost a few teeth and those that remain are quite worn down. So how old was Hornedjitef when he died? The evidence from his teeth and bones suggest that he was between 50 and 60 years old when he died. This was a good age to live to in ancient Egypt. Most people died before they were 40 years old.

The surfaces of these teeth are worn down, just like Hornedjitef's.

A painful disease

The scans also tell us about Hornedjitef's health and show that he had arthritis in his spine. Arthritis means that the joints between bones are painful. This happens to many people as they get older. The bones in the body start to get worn down and change shape. When we look at the scans of Hornedjitef's spine on page 25, we can see that the bones seem to go in at the middle. This is a sign of arthritis.

Jewelry and charms

Hornedjitef's titles tell us that he was an important man, a priest of very high status. His mummy might be expected to be made to a very high standard. Again, the CAT scans can help us find out about this. Inside the wrappings Hornedjitef is lying with his legs straight out and his arms folded across his ribs. There is a ring on a finger on his left hand and a wide plain ring on his left big toe. When a CAT scanner detects metal it leaves black marks around the object and if you look carefully at the scans you will see black marks around these finger and toe rings. This means they are probably made of gold. The embalmers put amulets among the wrappings, and many of these can be seen on Hornedjitef's chest and near his neck.

Many of the CAT scans were put together to make this three-dimensional image of Hornedjitef's chest. Inside you can see his lungs (colored blue), which have been wrapped and placed back in the body. His heart has been colored red. At the front his arms are folded and there is a ring (colored orange) on his left hand.

If you look carefully at the scan on page 35, you can see a large oval shape under his left shoulder. This is Hornedjitef's **heart scarab**. It seems to have slipped.

A well-made mummy

The embalmers sometimes put the internal organs they removed in special **canopic jars**, but at the time when Hornedjitef was mummified the organs were usually put back into the body after being wrapped in salt and linen. On the scans of Hornedjitef's mummy there are long packages inside the stomach and chest areas—these are his organs wrapped in linen and returned to the body.

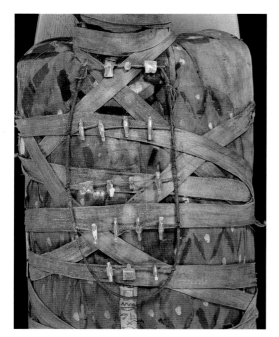

This mummy has amulets placed on top of the chest wrappings. Hornedjitef's are on his chest and all around his neck inside the wrappings (see page 35).

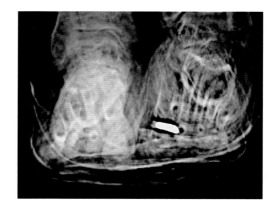

The CAT scans show that Hornedjitef is wearing a thick gold ring on the big toe of his left foot.

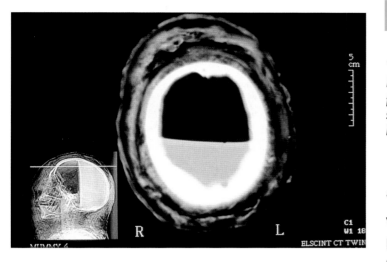

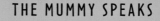

The scans show that after his brain was taken out Hornedjitef's skull was filled with resin. In the smaller picture you can see the solid resin at the back of his skull. In the larger picture you are looking down inside his skull. The resin is the dense white patch.

A mummy mugshot

What did Hornedjitef look like when he was alive? Luckily, the CAT scanner can help here. Some of the 246 X rays taken of the mummy can be put together to give us an idea of what he looked like. He is an old man. He has a fleshy nose, large lips, and quite large ears. His eyes are closed and he looks calm and peaceful.

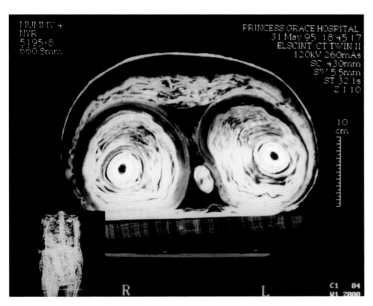

This CAT scan shows Hornedjitef's legs. Each leg was wrapped separately, then covered with a large sheet of linen. In the middle of each package you can see his leg bones.

The scans also show that Hornedjitef's brain was taken out and that his skull was half filled with resin.

Hornedjitef's body was wrapped in many layers of linen. The embalmers must have taken a lot of care with his body because his legs were first wrapped separately and then covered in larger sheets of linen. All the evidence shows that Hornedjitef's body was treated with respect and mummified to the highest standard. This is exactly what might be expected for a man with such an important job in ancient Egypt.

Many scans were put together to make a three-dimensional image of Hornedjitef's head. The image looks jagged at the edges because there are spaces between the scans. The top of his head could not be scanned because of the way his head lies to one side.

8 Waiting in eternity: Preparing for the afterlife

The mummy of Hornedjitef covered with decorated cartonnage and his mask.

After Hornedjitef's mummy was finally wrapped it was time for it to be decorated. The mummy was covered by a **cartonnage case** from his shoulders down to his feet. Cartonnage was made from layers of linen and wet plaster pressed together until it dried solid, a little like the papier mâché students use at school. When it was dry the surface was covered with scenes often seen on earlier Egyptian mummies. The scenes are religious ones, showing various gods protecting the mummy on its journey to the afterlife. They are gilded, with a green, blue, and red background. A huge collar in gold and dark blue stripes crosses the chest of the case. On the soles of his feet there are painted pictures of two prisoners with their hands tied behind their back. This is a scene often shown on Egyptian mummies and at the base of statues. It meant that Egypt was powerful and that any enemies of the country would be caught and tied up. It also meant that the mummy would fight off anybody who tried to stop him reaching the afterlife.

Hornedjitef's mummy with the mask taken off to show his linen-wrapped head.

Hornedjitef's cartonnage mummy mask, which shows him eternally young.

These bound prisoners are carved at the bottom of a gigantic statue of the pharaoh Ramesses II outside his temple at Abu Simbel.

Two tied-up prisoners are painted on the soles of Hornedjitef's feet. This gives the idea that Hornedjitef will tread on enemies who try to harm his beloved country—Egypt.

A separate gilded cartonnage mask was placed over Hornedjitef's head. This is also decorated with religious scenes to protect the mummy. The face modeled on the mask is that of a young man but Hornedjitef was not a young man—he was at least 50 years old. Like all Egyptians, including the elderly lady Katebet on page 37, Hornedjitef hoped to be reborn as a young man in the next life. So he had had his mask modeled as a young-looking man with golden skin. The mask originally had a curled beard but this was lost a long time ago. The painted straps to hold it on can still be seen down the sides of his face. The large dark eyes of the mask look eagerly into the afterlife and we can feel his excitement and expectation.

Detail of the lid of the inner coffin, showing a winged scarab beetle and baboons worshipping the sun.

The inner coffin

The mummy was then placed in the first of two coffins. This first coffin is his inner coffin and it is made of **sycamore** wood. It is richly painted and gilded on the outside. Many coffins made during the Ptolemaic period had a large **pectoral** on the chest and we can see one here. (There was another one on the mummy itself.) The inner coffin also has a huge collar, made to look like colored flowers. On the ends of the necklace by Hornedjitef's shoulders are falcon heads, to remind the mummy of the god Horus. In the middle of the lid is a scarab beetle with wings and a sun disc. Eight baboons are standing on the scarab's wings, greeting the sun. Beneath the scarab beetle are rows of hieroglyphs going down toward his feet. Again Hornedjitef's face is the golden face of a young man and this time his braided beard (with chin straps) has survived. Here Hornedjitef is wearing a large black wig.

The lid of Hornedjitef's inner coffin.

The inside of the lid of the inner coffin, with a picture of the goddess Nut.

At the bottom of the inner coffin Anubis guards the mummy.

Part of the inside of the inner coffin lid, showing scenes of the zodiac.

The hypocephalus— a device to keep the mummy warm.

The inside of the lid of the inner coffin shows a picture of the sky-goddess, Nut, with her hands stretched above her head. To Nut's left is a list of planets and stars. These stars rose in the sky every ten days and helped the Egyptians tell the time. On Nut's right are **constellations** and protective gods. Zodiac scenes such as this were often used in tombs in earlier periods, the most famous one being that of King Sety I (1294–1279 BC) of the 19th Dynasty. Written on Nut's body is Chapter 89 of the **Book of the Dead**. At the bottom of this lid, where the mummy's feet rested, you can see the jackal god Anubis, as always guarding the mummy on its journey to the next life.

Part of Hornedjitef's Book of the Dead, telling him how to get to the afterlife.

Keeping warm

Before the lid of the inner coffin was fitted onto its base something was put under the head of the mummy inside. This was a **hypocephalus** made of hardened and decorated linen. The decoration showed chapter 162 of the Book of the Dead and gave the mummy warmth.

The scroll of instructions

Henry Salt's assistant Giovanni d'Athenasi wrote that when he opened the outer coffin to get to the inner coffin and mummy he found a papyrus roll lying on the lid of the inner coffin. He said the papyrus was in very good condition and was 18 inches in height and 16 feet in length. Soon after the papyrus was brought to the British Museum in 1835 it was cut into smaller pages to make it easier to handle. The papyrus also contains chapters from the Book of the Dead that were meant to give the mummy instructions on how to get to the afterlife. The papyrus is written in **hieratic** script. In the sale of Mr Salt's collection this papyrus was bought for about $140.

Front view of the enormous black outer coffin.

The wooden chest holding Hornedjitef's canopic jars.

The bottom part of the outer coffin. The goddess Nut will protect the mummy of Hornedjitef.

The outer coffin

Many coffins made during the Ptolemaic period are massive in size and are very wide. Hornedjitef's outer coffin is just like this. The inner coffin was placed inside the enormous outer coffin, which has yellow decorations painted on a black background. It looks very strong and powerful. Another picture of the goddess Nut is shown on the base of the outer coffin. Here she is lying with her hands faced upward. Like Anubis, she is protecting the mummy. Both the inner and outer coffins are designed in the shape of the human body. Coffins shaped like this are known as anthropoid coffins.

When Hornedjitef's tomb was found it also contained a canopic chest to keep his canopic jars. This wooden chest is now in Leiden, Holland. Often the organs taken out of a body were put in canopic jars, but Hornedjitef's organs had been put back in his body. The CAT scans showed long packages inside his chest and abdomen area. So why did Hornedjitef need a canopic chest to hold his organs if his organs were in his body? A mystery? When the museum in Leiden looked inside the packages in the canopic chest they found only pieces of broken pots and no internal organs! It seems that the embalmers put the canopic chest in Hornedjitef's tomb because it was the traditional thing to do.

The god of the dead

The final object from Hornedjitef's tomb was a wooden statue of a god known as Ptah-Sokar-Osiris, one of the forms of the god of the dead. From the time of the 18th Dynasty a rolled-up copy of the Book of the Dead was often put into a compartment in the base of these statues. Hornedjitef's wooden statue has a compartment with a small rolled-up package in it. We already know that he also had a much larger and fuller Book of the Dead lying on his inner coffin.

Wooden statue of the god Ptah-Sokar-Osiris with a special compartment for a tiny rolled-up papyrus.

This papyrus shows a ceremony called the Opening of the Mouth.

The Opening of the Mouth

Priests such as Hornedjitef worked in temples but there were also very important things for priests to do at a person's funeral. On the day of Hornedjitef's burial his family and **mourners** collected his mummy and went to the tomb in a procession led by a priest. On the way a lector-priest chanted prayers and spells to make sure Hornedjitef reached the afterlife safely. The mourners would remember Hornedjitef when he was alive and women would throw dust over themselves to show how sad they were. The most important ceremony for Hornedjitef happened just before his burial. This was the **Opening of the Mouth** ceremony when the *sem*-priest in his exotic cat-skin touched Hornedjitef's mouth with various tools. This helped Hornedjitef to speak when questioned at the judgment by the gods.

Hornedjitef's mummy was placed in his tomb. His **grave goods** were placed around him. The tomb was closed up and Hornedjitef started his journey to the afterlife.

45

9 Hornedjitef: The mystery solved?

As we leave Hornedjitef traveling to the afterlife, what have we learned about his life and how his body was prepared after death?

Many young students, like Nicole and Isabelle, are interested in finding out more about Hornedjitef for themselves.

Hornedjitef grew up in Thebes on the banks of the Nile River and did the same things as other boys. He may have swum in the river and caught fish, played games, and gone around with his friends. Unlike some boys, however, he had the opportunity to go to school. Here he learned to read and write. This meant that he could become a priest when he grew up. He must have been very successful in his job because he was given a great deal of responsibility as a priest of the god Amun. The king rewarded him with wealth and important titles.

He lived to a ripe old age and when he died he had an expensive funeral. He could afford to have his body mummified to a high standard. He was also wealthy enough to have some beautifully made objects in his tomb.

Perhaps Hornedjitef has one or two more secrets that you might like to find out for yourself?

The British Museum bought the mummy of Hornedjitef, his two coffins, and the other objects from his tomb from Henry Salt. Giovanni d'Athanasi, who worked with Henry Salt, wrote that he was worried about mummies and their grave goods being separated and sent to different places. Luckily, apart from the canopic chest (which is in Leiden, Holland) this did not happen to Hornedjitef. His mummy, papyrus, hypocephalus, Ptah-Soker-Osiris statue, and coffins are now reunited in the British Museum.

Today the mummy and grave goods are displayed together in a new showcase. Thousands of visitors have been to see Hornedjitef already. Perhaps you would like to visit him one day and continue this investigation for yourself?

Glossary

abattoir — place where animals are killed and cut up for meat.

abdomen — part of the body containing the stomach and intestines.

amulets — good luck charms.

archaeologists — people who study the peoples and places of the past.

bacteria — tiny organisms that can cause disease or make a body decay.

Book of the Dead — spells written on a papyrus roll to help the deceased reach the Afterlife. The papyrus roll was put in the tomb with the mummy.

canopic jars — pots or containers with a stopper. The internal organs taken from mummified bodies were sometimes put inside them.

cartonnage case — cover fitting around the mummy, made of hard layers of painted linen.

CAT scanning — Computerized Axial Tomography. A kind of X ray that makes a map of the body from top to bottom using a computer to record the information.

cemetery — place where dead bodies are buried.

constellation — group of stars in the sky.

decree — order or rules given by an important person such as a king.

Delta — northern part of Egypt where the Nile River breaks up into smaller streams before reaching the sea.

descendants — children, grandchildren, great-grandchildren (and so on).

Egyptology — the study of objects from ancient Egypt.

embalming — making a mummy. Embalmers are people who do this work.

excavation — describes the places where archaeologists dig looking for information about past times.

ferment — to use yeast to make a liquid bubble up and become alcoholic. The Egyptians used yeast in bread to make beer.

funerary mask — cartonnage cover placed on a mummy's face before it was buried.

gesso — plaster mixed with glue. Gesso can be used as a surface for writing or painting.

grave goods — objects such as pottery and jewelry put in a grave or tomb with a dead body.

gypsum — plaster-like substance.

heart scarab — stone carved in the shape of a scarab beetle, put near a mummy's heart as a good luck charm.

hypocephalus — disc of hardened linen decorated with spells, put under a mummy's head to keep it warm.

Lower Egypt — the northern part of Egypt.

monuments — statues, temples, tombs, and other important structures.

mourners — people who go to a funeral to say goodbye to the dead person.

New Kingdom — period of Egyptian history between 1550 and 1069 BC.

Old Kingdom — period of Egyptian history between 2686 and 2181 BC.

Opening of the Mouth — ceremony in ancient Egypt when a priest touched the mummy's mouth with a tool to allow the mummy to speak when it meets the gods.

papyrus — kind of tall reed, used to make things such as sandals, boats, and writing paper.

pectoral — ornament worn on the chest.

pelvic bones — hip bones.

plaque — piece of metal, wax, or wood. To keep out evil spirits embalmers sometimes put one over the cut they made in a mummy.

predynastic period — time in Egyptian history before the names of kings and queens were written down.

Ptolemaic period — time when Egypt was ruled by Greek kings called Ptolemy. There were 14 kings called Ptolemy.

resin — liquid from plants that dries very hard.

Roman period — period in Egyptian history between 30 BC and 395 AD when the Romans ruled Egypt.

scarab beetle — Egyptian beetle that lives and lays eggs in dung. The Egyptians admired it because it works very hard.

shrine — holy place where religious objects are kept.

sycamore — type of fig tree grown in Egypt and other parts of the Middle East.

tomb — building made of stone or mud brick for a dead person.

Upper Egypt — southern part of Egypt. Thebes (modern Luxor) is in this area.

Further reading

Carol Donoughue, *The Mystery of the Hieroglyphs*, Oxford University Press, New York, 1999.

George Hart, *Eyewitness: Ancient Egypt*, Dorling Kindersley, New York, 2000.

Delia Pemberton, *Egyptian Mummies: People from the Past*, Harcourt, New York, 2001.

Stuart Smith and Nancy Bernard, *Valley of the Kings*, Oxford University Press, New York, 2002.